Cross, Resurrection, And Ascension

*First Lesson Sermons
For Lent/Easter
Cycle A*

Richard Gribble

CSS Publishing Company, Inc., Lima, Ohio

CROSS, RESURRECTION, AND ASCENSION

Copyright © 1998 by
CSS Publishing Company, Inc.
Lima, Ohio

All rights reserved. No part of this publication may be reproduced in any manner whatsoever without the prior permission of the publisher, except in the case of brief quotations embodied in critical articles and reviews. Inquiries should be addressed to: Permissions, CSS Publishing Company, Inc., P.O. Box 4503, Lima, Ohio 45802-4503.

Scripture quotations are from the *New Revised Standard Version of the Bible*, copyright 1989 by the Division of Christian Education of the National Council of the Churches of Christ in the USA. Used by permission.

Paraphrased stories from John Aurelio, *Colors! Stories of the Kingdom* © 1993. Used with permission of The Crossroad Publishing Company, New York.

Paraphrase of "Lily" from Walter Wangerin, Jr., *Ragman and Other Cries of Faith* © 1984. Used by permission of HarperCollins Publishers.

Library of Congress Cataloging-in-Publication Data

Gribble, Richard.
   Cross, Resurrection, and Ascension : first lesson sermons for Lent/Easter. Cycle A / Richard Gribble.
     p. cm.
   ISBN 0-7880-1229-0
   1. Lenten sermons. 2. Easter—Sermons. 3. Bible. O.T.—Sermons. 4. Catholic Church—Sermons. 5. Sermons, American. I. Title.
BV4277.G74   1998
252'.62—dc21   98-5113
                                                                                           CIP

This book is available in the following formats, listed by ISBN:
   0-7880-1229-0   Book

PRINTED IN U.S.A.

This book is dedicated to my two sisters, Judy and Barbara, with whom I was raised, learned the precepts of the Faith, and began the Christian journey from the desert, to the tomb, to resurrection, and ascension.

Table Of Contents

Introduction	7
Ash Wednesday The Journey To Freedom Begins Joel 2:1-12, 12-17	9
Lent 1 Greed Leads To Destruction Genesis 2:15-17; 3:1-7	13
Lent 2 Answering God's Call To Mission Genesis 12:1-4a	17
Lent 3 The Water of Life Exodus 17:1-7	21
Lent 4 Looking To The Heart 1 Samuel 16:1-13	25
Lent 5 Moving From Death To Life Ezekiel 37:1-14	31
Passion/Palm Sunday The Mission Of Christ is Ours Isaiah 50:4-9a	37
Maundy Thursday Carrying On The Tradition Exodus 12:1-4 (5-10) 11-14	41

Good Friday 45
    Freely Sharing The Burden
    Isaiah 52:13—53:12

Easter 49
    Our Need To Talk With The Son
    Acts 10:34-43

Easter 2 53
    A Resumé For Resurrection
    Acts 2:14a, 22-32

Easter 3 57
    Metanoia: The Process Of Conversion
    Acts 2:14a, 36-41

Easter 4 61
    Community Forms The Common Good
    Acts 2:42-47

Easter 5 65
    Proclaiming The Message Of God
    Acts 7:55-60

Easter 6 69
    Center Yourself In The Lord
    Acts 17:22-31

Ascension Of The Lord 73
    Completing The Master's Work
    Acts 1:1-11

Easter 7 77
    The Community Of Life
    Acts 1:6-14

Introduction

Lent and Easter are seasons of preparation and praise where the culmination of the powerful story of Salvation History is dramatically retold through the Scriptures and liturgical expression. Lent is the period when we make preparations in our lives, as individuals and community, for the great events of Holy Week. We enter a journey that takes us from the desert, to the cross, to resurrection. We begin this journey of preparation through an invitation on Ash Wednesday to return to the Lord with our whole hearts. We are reminded that this season must be a period to reflect on our lives, honestly evaluate what we find, and make efforts to correct problems and errors. We are asked to use this time to pray more, consider penance, and fast. It is a season when we must also look outward, observe the needs of our world, and act to correct the wrongs and injustices that we see. Lent is a period of six weeks of preparation to ready ourselves and the Christian community for the celebration of the paschal mystery — the passion, death, and resurrection of the Lord. We need this season of grace to look into our hearts, straighten out our priorities as needed, and walk more closely with the Lord. We cannot possibly celebrate the joy of the resurrection without suffering through the agony of Good Friday.

Easter is our celebration of Christ's triumph over death which provided the possibility of salvation for all people. We profess our alleluia song that Jesus has won for us the pearl of great price, our salvation and eternal life with God, for which all must be sacrificed. In the Scriptures we hear about the beginnings of the Christian community, which struggled but triumphed with the knowledge that the hand of God was leading and gently guiding its movements. Jesus leaves the apostles with his message of love and peace as he ascends to the Father from whom he came.

Preachers have the awesome, often difficult, but always privileged and important task of making the word of God come alive and become relevant for those whom we serve in ministry. The Scriptures must inspire us to be able to share what we have been given with others. The church becomes a classroom and the pulpit our lectern from which preachers have the opportunity and responsibility to teach. They become in a very real sense educators in the faith. The task of preaching is not easy. Thus, one commissioned by the community with this awesome responsibility must be ever diligent in efforts to proclaim faithfully and fearlessly God's message. This is the preachers' call as ministers to God's people.

This book moves from the desert of Ash Wednesday, to the cross of Calvary on Good Friday, to the empty tomb on Easter, and finally to Jesus' return to the Father. These homilies represent my journey which I wish to share with others. I am hopeful that they will inspire readers in their preaching efforts so that they may share God's love with those to whom they minister. I pray that the fire of God's love present in the Scriptures will set our hearts aflame to carry His message throughout these holy seasons of Lent and Easter.

Richard Gribble, CSC

Ash Wednesday

The Journey To Freedom Begins

Joel 2:1-2, 12-17

Mohandas Gandhi, the famous Indian freedom fighter and certainly one of the most influential personalities of the twentieth century, was born into a working-caste family in 1869. After he completed his initial education in India he went to England and entered law school. With his degree in hand Gandhi returned to his native land in the mid-1890s but was unable to find a fulfilling position. He received an invitation via a friend to go to South Africa to practice law, but more especially to be an advocate for the small Indian community there which was suffering discrimination at the hands of the ruling class. He accepted the challenge, went to South Africa, and in the process discovered his vocation. For twenty years Gandhi led the drive of the Indian people to achieve dignity and their rightful place in society. The tools he used to achieve his desired end were not those of a typical emancipator. He chose non-violent protest, civil disobedience, as his chief weapon. Dialogue and negotiation, respect, even love were additional tools he used to achieve his goals. He developed a whole system of non-violent protest which he called *satyagraha* or truth-force. His alternative methods were successful; the people reclaimed their dignity and took their rightful place in South African society.

In 1914 Gandhi again returned to India. World War I had just erupted on the European continent. England, India's overseer, was fully involved in the worldwide conflict and at this time Gandhi supported its efforts. After the war, however, things changed. In 1919 at Amristar over 300 Indian nationals were ruthlessly and senselessly murdered by British soldiers as the people peacefully protested England's domination of their country. The incident galvanized the attitude of the people and it changed Gandhi's opinion of the British and their presence in India forever. For the next 25 years Gandhi led India's drive for freedom from the British. As with his campaign in South Africa, the tools Gandhi used were different than any revolutionary leader before him. He substituted words for bullets, offered respect in place of hate, and promoted the use of marches and civil disobedience in place of armed aggression.

Mohandas Gandhi suffered a great deal because of his alternative approach. He fasted on several occasions, sometimes for many days, to alert the world to the plight of his people. He was incarcerated by British officials many times totaling more than six years. Yet, ultimately in 1947 India gained its freedom. The might and grandeur of the British Empire had been brought to its knees by a little, almost unnoticeable man, and it was done without one bullet being fired. It was a different approach, not one which society valued, but it was effective in achieving its end. Although Gandhi led his nation to freedom, his life was sacrificed. In January 1948, only a few months after the British exodus, Gandhi was felled by an assassin's bullet as he walked to prayer. The man of peace was silenced by one calculated act of violence.

Today we begin the discipline of Lent, our annual journey from the wilderness of the desert, to the wood of the cross, and finally to the freedom of the empty tomb. As Gandhi led the Indian people to freedom using alternate tools, ones not well respected by society, so the Church leads her people to freedom, and the methods used are not conventional.

The prophet Joel wrote to the Hebrew people after their return from fifty years of exile in Babylon. The people knew what it meant to return home physically; it was now time for them to return in spirit, to come home to God. Joel first speaks of the need all people have to return to God. In our hearts and minds we must make the turn away from the world and toward God. Before the journey can begin in earnest we must set our direction straight.

The tools needed for our journey home to God are different than those required for a more conventional trip. The prophet first says that we must fast. Fasting requires us to discipline ourselves, a necessity for the journey which we begin this day. We deny ourselves some of the pleasures of food, as did Jesus in the desert, to remind us that this is a special time of preparation. Fasting, however, is more than self-denial; it is also the discipline of acceptance and accommodation. The liturgical environment will change, as will our weekly celebration in our church, in order to remind us of the journey we begin. Some people do not like change, even for short periods, but through the discipline we develop in fasting we gain the strength for acceptance.

Joel next tells us that we must rend our hearts — we must seek reconciliation. When Jesus told the parable of the Prodigal Son he spoke of reconciliation as a journey which requires us to achieve forgiveness on three levels. First, we must learn to forgive ourselves. The younger (prodigal) son realized that he had done wrong and that his return home was the only answer. His ability to find reconciliation within himself allowed him to seek the forgiveness of others. The older brother, unfortunately, gives us a negative example of his inability to forgive others, which is the necessary second step in our reconciliation journey. Like a weak link in a chain which snaps and destroys the chain's usefulness, so the elder son's inability to forgive stunts the process of reconciliation. The younger son, however, does achieve reconciliation with his father, whose forgiveness has been present from the moment the boy made the decision to return home. Joel challenges us to begin this process of reconciliation in our return to the Lord.

The prophet also encourages the people, and we who live today as well, to assemble, pray as a community, and begin to change. We come to church; we gather as God's people today to start our journey to freedom. We walk this sometimes windy and treacherous road armed with the gifts of God, unconventional by the standards of the world, but mightier and of greater assistance than anything the world can provide. On Ash Wednesday we gather as a Christian community in prayer to initiate our preparation for the paschal mystery — the passion, death, and resurrection of the Lord.

Our ultimate goal of freedom, which the empty tomb brings, can only be achieved by our preparation now for the journey which follows. Certain signs will guide us in our use of the special tools of fasting, reconciliation, and prayer which Joel gives us today. Ashes, made from the burnt palms of last year's Passion Sunday celebration, are placed on our foreheads as a sign of where we have come from and where we will one day return. This sacramental act also helps us to see that we must "repent and believe in the Good News." The color purple is used in our liturgical environment also to remind us again of the journey we begin and its central message of reconciliation. We are in a time of preparation for the freedom which only God can give; thus our celebration is somewhat subdued. In this way we can learn more about the power and symbolism of silence.

Freedom is an elusive goal. We live in the United States as free people governed by a democratic system of laws, yet in certain ways, possibly without our knowing, we are chained to the world as assuredly as a prisoner is shackled to iron bars. The world says that the solutions to conflict, disagreements, and the myriad of human problems can only be found in the answers which society provides. Human solutions can provide a respite and temporary relief, but they cannot bring us to true freedom. It is only through death and our return to God that we will truly be free. We need to make this forty-day journey with Jesus, as he walked, prayed, and fasted in the desert. Our tools for the trip are unconventional — reconciliation, fasting, and prayer, but like those used by Mohandas Gandhi in his fight for freedom for his people, the tools given us by God will achieve their purpose of preparing us fully for the Easter mystery. Let us, therefore, begin the journey from the desert, to the cross, to freedom. It is a challenging mission but its ultimate goal — eternal life — is worth our best effort.

Lent 1

Greed Leads To Destruction

Genesis 2:15-17; 3:1-7

Once there was a man who owned a little plot of land. It wasn't much by the world's standards, but it was enough for him. He was a busy man who worked very hard, and for enjoyment he decided to plant a garden on his plot of land. First he grew flowers with vibrant colors which gave promise of spring and later fragrant flowers which graced the warm summer days. Still later he planted evergreens that spoke of life in the midst of a winter snow. Over the years the man continued to embellish his special little garden, at one time planting trees that offered shade and beauty and at another digging a small pond where his children could play. Finally, on the little land that was left he built a gazebo where he and his wife could relax on the warm summer evenings. It was not much, but it was his special little garden.

One day the man's next-door neighbor died and left him his property. It was a plot much larger than his own and he began to dream of all the possibilities that this new land might afford him. He made big plans which included hedgegrows and groves, arbor trees, and vine-covered trellises. He would build a huge pond for swimming in the summer and ice skating in the winter. His dreams became extravagant, but he set himself to the task with full resolve. The little garden continued to grow, which took time to manage, time that was very precious now with all the work and plans for the development of his newly-acquired land. He had less and less time to enjoy the garden with his family, but he consoled himself by thinking that there would be time enough when the new project was finished. Yet, if he was going to do it, he was determined to do it right. Thus, he figured he needed a winding cobblestone road and a special fieldstone wall around the new plot of land. A simple pond would no longer suffice; nothing short of a large lake would be sufficient. This would require additional land, so he bought more.

His new investment in land necessitated that he build a larger and more fitting residence, a manor house for his growing estate. There must be a carriage house for cars and a gate house for decor. All of this work was too much for him so he hired a team of laborers to assist him in his grand project. In order to pay the workers, he was required to work even harder and longer.

Unfortunately the man overextended himself. With his energy drained and resources exceeded, the work stopped. The fence was left unfinished; the lake became a swamp; the garden was soon overgrown. In his waning years the man sat alone in his broken-down gazebo and dreamed of a little plot of land. He didn't need very much, just enough for him to plant a special little garden.[1]

The man was not satisfied with the garden he possessed. It was beautiful and sufficient for his needs, but he continued to want more. His greed caused him to overextend himself, and in the end he lost everything and longed for the simple garden which he originally had. On this the first Sunday in Lent we hear a familiar story in our Old Testament lesson which gives us a challenge to avoid greed at all costs.

God created the Garden of Eden to be the perfect environment for His greatest creation, the human race. Nothing was left out of God's plan; everything that the man and woman would need was there and available to them. God gave the couple instructions on how they were to live in this idyllic paradise. Satan, in the form of a serpent, however, convinced the woman that she needed more than she already possessed. Her sin appears at our first reading to be disobedience to God's command. She ate the fruit from the tree of which God had forbidden her, and convinced her mate to do likewise. The woman disobeyed God, but her downfall was greed; she wanted something that she didn't have, a fruit which had been denied her. She did not need the fruit; there was plenty of other food all around. Yet we read, "The woman saw that the tree was good for food, and that it was a delight to the eyes, and that the tree was to be desired to make one wise" (3:6a). She wanted to become like God. In the process, however, she lost everything and the man as well. The knowledge that they gained was not the wisdom of God as they had been told; they learned only of their nakedness and loss of innocence.

The man and woman, Adam and Eve as Genesis later calls them, like the man with the garden, were greedy, extended their holdings too far, and lost everything in the process. Certainly their fault has been and continues to be realized in our world. Napoleon in the nineteenth century and Adolf Hitler in the twentieth were not content to rule their own domains of France and Germany respectively; they could only be content with conquest of vast regions, a decision which led to their demise as well. How often today we hear of businesses that expand, diversify, and purchase smaller establishments only to have the economy shift, which leads to failure to the chagrin of management and workers alike. The gambler too is seldom content with winning one sum; greed enters, the person risks what was won and in the end loses all that was gained.

Power, wealth, and prestige, the three great temptations of our world, can corrupt us if we place our emphasis on them and not on the greater gifts of God. The woman was tempted in this way. The serpent offered her the wealth of a good tree with delectable fruit and the power and prestige of being like God. The temptation was too great and she faltered. We too are almost daily tempted, sometimes in subtle and other times in more obvious ways, with the allure of power, wealth, and prestige. We have the daily challenge to use our God-given multiple and varied gifts for constructive purposes to aid others and build the Kingdom of God in our world. Greed and selfishness lead to abuse of these gifts and enslavement to power, wealth, and prestige. If we become self-centered and, like the man in the story, through greed build our garden without thought of others or what is necessary for the task, then most assuredly we will lose what we have gained. God is the one who casts down the mighty from their thrones and lifts up the lowly. Jesus in the Scriptures challenges us to be satisfied with what we need and refuse the allure of our many desires. God will give us all that we need; it will never be denied us. As we begin in earnest our Lenten journey this first Sunday, let us pray that God will strengthen us to avoid greed and the allurements of the world experienced in power, wealth, and prestige. Let us use wisely the gifts and talents we have been given to bring praise and glory to God — the Father, Son, and Holy Spirit.

---

1. Paraphrased from "A Special Little Garden," in John Aurelio, *Colors! Stories of the Kingdom* (New York: The Crossroad Publishing Company, 1993), pp. 150-151.

Lent 2

Answering God's Call To Mission

Genesis 12:1-4a

On a warm and sunny early June day in 1943 John Francis Laboon, "Jake" to his friends, stood with his Naval Academy classmates on Worden Field; it was graduation day. These men were the class of 1944, but because of the war raging in both the Pacific and European theatres, and thus the need for its services in the fleet, the class was "accelerated" one year in its training. A rough and tumble young man from the steel town of Pittsburgh, Jake had come to the Academy in the summer of 1940. He excelled in athletics during his tenure, earning the honor of an All-East selection as tight end on the Academy's football team and leading the lacrosse squad, by his selection as an All-American defenseman, to the national championship in 1943.

The athletic heroics and even the regimen of the Academy had to be put away, however, as it was not only graduation day, but the date each member of the class was to be commissioned as an officer in the Navy or Marine Corps. Jake and his classmates raised their right hands and took the oath of office from the Secretary of the Navy, pledging themselves to service of country and "to defend and protect the Constitution of the United States." Jake had trained for this moment for three years, academically, professionally, physically, and spiritually. Now was the hour for him to accept his commission, apply the talents and gifts he had nurtured and acquired, and do the work for which he had been trained. He knew not where his commission would take him, but he accepted with faith that if he carried out his duty his efforts would be rewarded and recognized.

After graduation Jake reported to the Naval Submarine School in New London, Connecticut. When this short training period ended, he traveled west to Pearl Harbor and was assigned to the *USS Peto*. As a junior officer he served well, completing five war patrols, and winning the silver star for gallantry when he rescued a downed naval aviator in Japanese waters. In June 1946 Jake was transferred from the *Peto*. Three months later, with the whole US military in standdown after the war, he resigned his commission in the Navy. The Lord was calling Jake Laboon to another commission with its uncertainty and the probability that it would require him again to change and go where God called.

Jake contemplated the diocesan priesthood for a couple of years, but, in response to God's call, entered the Jesuit novitiate at Woodstock, Maryland, in 1949. He was ordained a priest in 1956 and two years later completed a doctorate in theology. Uncertain as to the ministry he desired, Jake reached out for God's guiding hand and heard the call to return to the Navy as a chaplain. After securing the permission of his religious superiors, Jake reentered the service with its life of uncertainty and travel. Beginning with his first duty station at Patuxent River Naval Air Station in Maryland, Jake Laboon served an illustrious career as a Navy chaplain. He traveled far and wide and met many people. Some of his most noteworthy duty stations were a return to his alma mater, the Naval Academy, from 1966-1969, chaplain to the staff of the Commander-in-Chief Pacific Fleet from 1972-1975, and just before his retirement in 1980, service as force chaplain for the Commander-in-Chief Atlantic Fleet.

Upon retirement Jake took up a new commission when he joined the Jesuit retreat house staff at Manresa on the Severn in Annapolis. With the Naval Academy visible from his bedroom window, Jake Laboon touched the hearts of thousands as a retreat master and confessor. In 1988 he was assigned as pastor of St. Alphonsus Church in Woodstock, Maryland. There, after a short illness, he died. Because of his wide-reaching and important assignments, as well as his dedication and commitment to God and country, Jake Laboon was without question the best known and most widely-respected chaplain in the US fleet. The commissioning of the *USS*

Laboon in 1993, only the second ship ever dedicated to the memory of a chaplain, demonstrates his greatness and the appreciation of others. Jake Laboon was a man who accepted his commission, went where the Lord asked him to go, applied his talents, and served God and country.

Jake Laboon followed his call from God, despite the distance from familiar territory, the changes which it required, or the fact that it might not have been his choice. His faithfulness to purpose, God, and country made him well-respected among his peers and gained him the admiration of many. On this the Second Sunday in Lent we hear how Abram was placed in a similar situation, demonstrated his faith, and in the process initiated God's plan of Salvation History for all people.

Abram's call from God was not expected. He was an obscure Semite who lived in a region east of the Jordan River, but God had special plans for him and his descendants. Abram was asked to dissociate himself from his pagan past, metaphorically to leave his kinsfolk and father's house. He was further challenged to migrate to a distant and foreign land under God's direction. God's commission to Abram was not easy; it required him to leave behind everything that he knew and to start over again. God did not ask obedience without a promise, however. The Lord promised Abram that he would be rewarded for his obedience. His name would be considered great and respected by all people; he would be the father of a great nation. All the world would find a special blessing in Abram.

God's challenge to Abram shifts the story of Genesis and initiates God's loving plan for all men and women, what theologians call Salvation History. It would be through Abram (later Abraham) and his descendants, God's chosen people, the Jews, that the Lord's master plan for the redemption of all people would be revealed. God chose Abram as a vehicle to initiate His plan that would find its fulfillment and climax in Jesus and the redemptive action of his life, and his passion, death, and resurrection. Abram's obedience to God's command was necessary so the human race could be released from the sin of Adam and Eve about which we heard last Sunday.

God calls us to go many places and do many things that may cause us to change, shift gears, or alter our plans. We may even be called to leave behind what we know and strike out in a new direction in life. In the journey of our working life we may be forced to relocate or to take up a different occupation. We may find ourselves in uncomfortable positions, where we feel our integrity or work ethic is jeopardized more often than we desire. In our families we also will be challenged by God. We may have to walk the road of ill-health with a spouse, a child, or other relative. Tough love may have to be exercised by us if we become involved with the addiction of another. We all will have to walk the road of death with someone close to us. Our lives of faith are not without challenges as well. God might not answer our prayers in the fashion or time we want, and the feeling that God has abandoned us may creep into our hearts. When someone special in our life ignores God and the Church and opts for the ways and things of the world we are again challenged.

Few of us in this life will have a task as great as Abram's, but we will all at different times be challenged to move from where we find ourselves to a new or higher realm. We must not be complacent; such an attitude leads only to stagnation. If we follow God's lead, if we place our trust in His providential guidance, then the Lord will safely lead us home.

Lent is a time to recast, reshape, and refocus our lives. We are on a journey that prepares us for the Easter mystery. We have all been commissioned through baptism to lead lives of holiness and service. During Lent we must look inside, honestly judge what we see, and then seek reconciliation and change in our lives. God's call will undoubtedly take us places we can only imagine today and ask us to perform tasks which seem impossible. If we have the courage of our convictions, that God is with us in all that we do and say, then the strength needed to persevere and continue on the road to God will be given to us. Let us today think of how Jake Laboon and Abram responded to God's call. They were challenged to forget their own desires and plans and do God's will in their lives. If we have the courage to do the same, our reward in heaven will be great.

Lent 3

The Water Of Life

Exodus 17:1-7

Knowledge that water is an integral ingredient of life was a concept not lost on the ancients. The great civilizations of the world located themselves near water and used it in most every aspect of their daily lives. The Egyptians built the world's first great empire along the Nile. In the midst of the desert a flourishing community existed and grew in size and strength. The water of the river provided the source of life for the people then as it does today. On both sides of the Nile a rich and fertile area exists for farming and grazing of livestock. Periodic floods enrich the land with the silt from the river bottom. Besides providing nourishment for crops and animals the river was the principal means of transportation, ferrying products and people to destinations north and south. In modern times the Nile is Egypt's main source of power generated at the Aswan Dam in the southern region of the nation.

The Egyptians were only the first of many peoples who understood the importance of water and the life it brought. Contemporaneous with the Egyptians, the Mesopotamians established a highly cultured and advanced civilization between the Tigris and Euphrates Rivers. Known as the Fertile Crescent, the area became home to the Babylonians, where the Hebrews would spend fifty years in exile. Throughout human history peoples have located themselves near water because of its life-giving qualities and aid in transportation. In our own country we can look to our history and note that most all great cities were established near some significant source of water.

Water has always been seen as a necessity for life. Greek philosophers, in their attempt to explain the world around them, proposed the idea that all matter was a composition of four basic elements: earth, fire, air, and water. All the visible things of the world contained some amount of water and were thus dependent upon it for their existence. Humans learned quickly that they could not long survive without water. The body can function without food for many days but not so without water. We use water to cleanse our world as well, whether that means washing our clothes, scrubbing the floor, or bathing ourselves.

The Hebrews, like the Egyptians and other ancients, understood the importance of water. From the setting described in today's reading from Exodus, water played an integral role in the life of the community. The "deliverer" Moses was saved from death when his mother placed him upon the waters and he was rescued from the river by Pharoah's daughter. God turned the waters of Egypt into blood in an attempt to convince Pharaoh to free the captive Hebrew nation. It was water that provided the escape path for the Israelites as they fled Egypt, and it was this same water which brought to ruin those who pursued the people as they escaped to the desert.

Water had in many ways brought the people to the desert, yet now we hear it is the lack of water which has generated a crisis in the Hebrew camp. Obviously the people needed water to meet their physical needs and the desert would prove a poor source, but the people seem to have forgotten that God had always provided for their needs in the past, especially in the recent past. The people think God has abandoned them and thus they grumble against God's servant Moses, the one drawn from the waters by God to lead the people to freedom. The people need the water, but they need God even more, and they cannot perceive it. The people fail to understand that God is the source of the water they so desperately need. Where can the people obtain water in the dry vast spaces of the desert; how can a rock bring forth water? The Hebrews miss the whole point of God's test; they failed to understand that God is the source of water. God is the source of all that they need. As David and other writers of the psalms would state generations later, God is the rock, the foundation of the people. God, their rock, can provide the living water the people need.

Like the people of earlier generations we need water to drink, for transportation, and to cleanse our world. Modern science has unlocked many of the mysteries of the miraculous qualities of water which allow us to understand our need for this ordinary substance which we often take for granted. But we also often find ourselves in the same dilemma as the Hebrews. Our needs are not met, the many "waters" of life are not satisfied, and we fail to seek God for solutions. As ancient philosophers believed water to be a part of all things, so we must understand and believe in the universal omnipresence of God. There is nothing in which God does not exist; there is no event wherein God is not present.

People have always needed water for transportation; we need God in the same way. There are many ways to get around, to travel from one place to another, but there is only one means of travel which will lead us to salvation. We need the providential hand of God to direct our often wayward lives back to the road that brings us to life. We can use so many other vehicles of society — addiction, escape from reality, or pleasure — to aid the thirst for our needs, the waters of life, but in the end all such solutions fall short, are found to be empty, and fail to satisfy.

Water was the great source of sustenance for the ancients and it continues to be for us today. We need all the physical properties which water provides, but we need God, the source of living water, more in the multiple ways that the Lord feeds us. The water which God provides is found in words, the Scriptures we read, sacrament, the bread of life we share, and what is most available yet seldom recognized, the presence of others. We know that water is integral to our lives; we cannot live long without it. In a similar and most important way God, the source of all good things, of living water, must be integral to our lives. We must drink of the Lord as assuredly as we drink water. Water nourishes our body; God nourishes our soul.

Lent is the perfect opportunity to refocus our sights on God, to realize anew our need for and dependence upon God. This is a season when we journey from the desert to the wood of the cross to the empty tomb. We will need to find water in the desert in order to continue our journey, and God will be the one who can provide this basic sustenance of life. We have many needs and equally as many if not more wants in our life. Water is one of the most basic needs of the body which must be satisfied in order to continue life. God is the source of life for the soul and the goal to which our life must be oriented. Let us continue to draw near to God. We will be sustained today, have our needs met, and brought to eternal life tomorrow.

Lent 4

Looking To
The Heart

1 Samuel 16:1-13

Once upon a time in a far-off land there lived a wise but old king. This monarch was very much beloved by his people, but alas he had no children, no heir to the throne. Because he did not want his kingdom to fall into the wrong hands after his death, the king decided to choose his own successor before he died. He had lived a long life and had done much reflection. He thought he knew what had gotten him to where he was and more importantly what would get his kingdom where it needed to be in the future. Therefore, he made a public decree that any person who thought himself qualified to be king should come to the capital city for an interview. The king's decree was promulgated throughout the land.

In a small village in that land, one young man heard about the decree and thought that he had the qualifications necessary to be king. He had good intelligence, was courageous, and understood the government. Unfortunately, the young man came from a poor family. He did not have the resources of money, clothes, and food to make the trip to the capital city. He was small of stature and was not impressive to those who saw him. Although he had many good qualities, the young man did not look like or possess the assets of one who wanted to be leader of the people. He decided that he should not make the trip; people would only laugh and jeer if he asked for an interview. His friends, however, encouraged him to set out telling him that all he needed would be provided on the trip. Therefore, he set out with some hesitation for the capital city to have his interview with the king. Along the way he was amazed to find that his friends were correct; all was provided for him. He was able to find lodging and a good hot meal each night in the village where he would stop. One family gave him a little money for those unexpected out-of-pocket expenses. Another family seeing his shabby clothes gave him a brand new suit for his audience with the king.

After several days' journey the young man reached a bridge which crossed over a mighty river which guarded the capital city on one side. As he was preparing to cross, a tired-looking old beggar man came up to him. "Please," said the old man, "may I have the extra food that you have? I live in the forest where food is at times hard to find. And, if possible can I have that fine new jacket you have? It is quite cold in the forest, and as you can see I have nothing to wear." The young man thought to himself, "I have come all this way and now this old man asks something of me." After he had thought about it for a few more minutes, however, he decided that the old man needed the things more than he did. Thus, he gave the old man his food and changed clothes with him, seeing that he needed more than just a coat. Nevertheless, not to be deterred from his quest, the young man crossed the bridge and entered the capital city.

When he reached the palace he was told that the king was away and could not see him until tomorrow. Thus, the young man waited outside the palace all night for his opportunity to be interviewed by the king. The next day, the young man was ushered into the palace by one of the guards. They passed down a long and beautiful hallway. The doors ahead of them opened unto the king's throne room; he was holding court. When the young man looked up, he was perplexed and somewhat confused. There on the throne was the same old man he had met on the bridge the previous day. The young man was angry and bewildered: "Why did you trick me?" asked the young man. "Why did you tell me you needed my food and clothes?" The king answered in a soft voice, "My son, I had heard from my royal officials that you were coming. You see, I do all of my interviews in the field. There is only one qualification for this job, to love and respect others; outside appearances mean nothing to me. I have judged your heart and you, my son, have passed the test. You will be the next king!"

The story of the boy who would became king illustrates many of the ideas which challenge us in our reading today. We hear how Samuel was sent to anoint a new king but he did not want the task; he feared Saul. With a little coaxing and advice from God, however, the prophet continued the mission as it was given to him. Samuel was quite impressed with Eliab, Jesse's eldest son. From what we can tell he looked like one who should be king; he was tall of stature, like Saul, manly, and courageous. Eliab's outer appearance was very impressive and it caused Samuel to conclude that he must be God's anointed. God, however, had a very different idea and taught Samuel a great lesson: "Do not look on his appearance or on the height of his stature, because I have rejected him; for the Lord does not see as mortals see; they look on the outward appearance, but the Lord looks on the heart" (1 Samuel 16:7). Jesse's seven eldest sons were paraded before Samuel, but none of them was selected by God. David, the youngest, was not even considered by Jesse; he did not look the part. He is described as ruddy, handsome, and with beautiful eyes. David was youthful, a boy in many ways, but God was able to see into his heart. God could see the potential which existed in David; the Lord could perceive the great leader that he would become.

In our lives we spend a lot of time and effort to improve our outward appearance. We run, lift weights, participate in aerobics, and many other physical activities to appear trim and fit. We are very conscious of our diet, watch calories and cholesterol, and eat those things which will keep us healthy. We groom our hair and wear clean and neat clothes to make ourselves attractive. Most of us spend a good number of years obtaining an education which will prepare us for excellence in the working world and impress others with our credentials. In short, we want our outside appearance to be the best it can be and our resumé to be attractive and complete. Contemporary society almost demands that we conform to this set of rules. If we choose another option or refuse to participate, the world will not choose us; we will be left behind. It is important to take care of ourselves and to make the most of our physical and intellectual abilities; a lesser effort would waste the gifts we have been given by God.

An important question, however, must be asked: how much effort do we put into the preparation, beautification, and strengthening of our spiritual self, our heart and soul, the place where God looks and judges? How often do we make a conscious effort to improve our spiritual life as we do so readily with our physical and intellectual appearance? If we fail to exercise, always eat poorly, refuse to challenge our minds, then most assuredly our outward appearance will not be attractive to those who see us. If we cannot find time for prayer, refuse to aid our fellow Christians in need, and forget our obligations as baptized people and thus members of God's family, then our spiritual appearance, the condition of our soul, will not be attractive to God, who, as Samuel was told, looks into the heart.

When we look at other people what do we see? Are we attracted by the three-piece suit, the designer dress, or the Gucci shoes or handbag? Do we see people for what they can bring us or how they can help us move up the ladder of society or business? What criteria do we use to select those with whom we will associate, those for whom we will vote, those who will gain our loyalty? Do we see only what is on the outside or can we look, as God suggests, into the heart?

All of us, if we are honest, spend a lot of time on outward appearances; we make judgments based on what we see and hear. God, however, tells us, as He told Samuel, that what is truly important is what is present in the heart. God reads the words of our heart and listens to the song of our soul. The Lord knows that the outside will change day to day and in the end pass away, but the heart is more permanent in its inaudible but nevertheless active voice.

It is certainly a wonderful reality for us that God sees the desire of our heart. The best Christian makes many mistakes, errors of life which are experienced on the outside. But since God created us and knows us, the desire of our heart is also known. God can see through the transitory elements of our life and grants forgiveness when we falter and fail to keep our Christian commitment. We must be willing to forgive others as God forgives us; we must look into the heart and not be fooled by the mutable outside appearance.

Lent is our time to take a new approach, to look beyond the obvious which outside appearances give and seek God's presence in the hearts of others. The king knew the heart of the young man; he experienced the desire of his soul during their encounter on the bridge where he conducted his interviews. Outside appearances did not fool the king; he knew where to look and he found his successor in the heart of the rags, poverty, youth, yet genuine goodness of the boy. Let us look into our heart and change as necessary to achieve a heart oriented toward God. Then let us turn our attention to others, look beyond what we see and hear, and concentrate on what God experiences in others. The task of the Christian life is always great; our response is awaited.

Lent 5

Moving From Death To Life

Ezekiel 37:1-14

He was chained, held bound in a life of torment and blasphemy. In the end, however, God would set him free. John Newton, a name probably not familiar to many people, was born in July 1725 to a pious English woman and her seafaring husband. From his earliest days, young Newton was attracted to his father's side of the family and to the life at sea. Thus, when he was only eleven years old he became an apprentice aboard his father's vessel, a cargo ship, which ferried products throughout the major ports of the Mediterranean region. To say the least, at this time in his life, John Newton did not know God. Those with whom he associated on his father's vessel were, for the most part, criminals, rogues, and other "undesirables" of society, many of whom were sent to Captain Newton's ship as punishment for some offense in the State of England.

When Newton was nineteen he became a midshipman on another vessel. After only one year, however, he was publicly flogged for insubordination. Despite this event, and most probably with the help of his father, John was able to secure a commission and a few years later his own vessel, a slave trading ship. John Newton commanded a vessel which ferried Africans from their native land to the American colonies. He was good at what he did; he carried out his duties fully and with precision. Yet, he felt chained to his life at sea, trapped and dead inside; he was unable to release himself.

This all changed one night in 1748. That evening while at sea Newton's slave ship was caught in a vicious storm. Waves crashed over the bow and the ship was tossed about like a toy. Through the skill of the captain and his crew, the ship and all personnel were saved. The experience, however, changed Newton forever. He felt the chains that held him bound begin to weaken; a new sense of spirit invaded his soul. It took seven more years, but finally in 1755 John Newton gave up the slave trade and his life at sea. That same year he met John Wesley and George Whitefield, two Anglican clergymen, who at that time were leaders in the evangelical revival which would lead to the foundation of Methodism in the United States. In 1764 Newton himself was ordained an Anglican priest. He became a well-known preacher and was one of the first members of what later became known as the Abolitionist movement, with such leaders as Daniel O'Connell in Ireland and William Lloyd Garrison in the United States. In 1779 Newton wrote some famous words, autobiographical in nature, that are familiar to us all: "Amazing grace, how sweet the sound that saved a wretch like me. I once was lost, but now I'm found, was blind but now I see." Yes, John Newton wrote the words to "Amazing Grace." He was held bound in a life he did not want; he experienced spiritual death. In the end, however, God was the one who set him free and granted him new life.

The experience of John Newton serves as a good example to illustrate an important point. Humans many times are trapped in situations that are not desired, bring no benefit, and often make us feel as if we are spiritually dead, without hope for any resolution to our problems. We try different solutions, varied ways to free ourselves, but in the end realize that God alone can free us and raise us to new life.

The prophecy of Ezekiel, which we hear in an almost mystical metaphorical passage in today's reading, was proclaimed to the Hebrews while they were in exile in Babylonia. The prophet brings a message of hope that a new spirit will come to Israel to allow the nation and its people to rise from death and find renewed hope in the future. The Hebrews, like John Newton, were dead inside and trapped by the circumstances of life; they could perceive no reason for future hope. God's messenger, however, proclaimed a new day for the Hebrews when they would rise from their graves and return to their home.

As we heard, Ezekiel is led by the Spirit of God onto a plain near Babylon, one which is strewn with the bones of those who have fallen in battle. On the plain the prophet has a mystical experience which symbolizes his mission as the bearer of hope to the Hebrew exiles. Dry bones, the lifeless remains of the human race which Ezekiel views spread across the land, represent the Hebrews in captivity. In extraordinary words of great power and image, he prophesies how these bones will rise again as a great army. The people had lost hope. We hear, "Our bones are dried up, and our hope is lost; we are cut off completely" (Ezekiel 37:11b). God, however, will bring a new day as the prophet relates: "I am going to open your graves, and bring you up from your graves, O my people; and I will bring you back to the land of Israel" (Ezekiel 37:12b). God will give the people a new start through a renewed spirit and they will be returned to their homeland.

Ezekiel prophesies how God will save the people, raise them to new life, give them a renewed spirit, and return them to the land. It will be necessary, however, that each person take personal responsibility in assuring that God's renewal of spirit will be used wisely to further the community in its path back home to God. God has given the people a new chance; it is now up to them to move forward and make something positive of this new opportunity to life.

Death is experienced in life in many ways, not simply the physical reality that all people will one day die. Like John Newton we are at times held captive by forces beyond our immediate control. We are weighed down, burdened, and trapped by things, people, and events. Although our heart is pumping and our brain operating, we feel dead in many ways and look for a solution to our dilemma. The physical death of family members, relatives, and friends causes us great grief. Death is always more difficult for those who are left behind. Sometimes when we experience the emotion of great sorrow, we wish we were the ones who had died; we die inside to some extent. In order to right our ship of life we seek a remedy or possibly a substitute for our grief. Disappointments in people and events, failures in life's tasks, and problems that seem unsolvable cause us to wonder if God has abandoned us, a feeling I am sure much like that of the Hebrews when they were in exile in Babylonia. We experience spiritual dryness and stagnation. We cannot find the time for prayer or it seems ineffective; we drift away from celebrating the Lord's day with the Christian community and see no reason to humble ourselves before God.

Injury, disease, or physical death, disappointment and failure, and spiritual emptiness are the dry lifeless bones of today's world. The pressures, tensions, and vicissitudes of life cause us to feel powerless against an unsympathetic, demanding, and goal-oriented world. We must find a way out; we must discover someone or something that can break the bonds that hold us bound in order to bring together the dry bones of our life and raise us to renewed life. Like John Newton we may not consciously seek a new direction and spirit, but we know things must change.

Lent is a journey where we have the opportunity to discover answers to the feelings of death that we experience in life. In moving from the desert to the cross to resurrection we come to realize that all our experiences of death were also felt by Jesus during his time on earth. During his public ministry he broke the bonds of slavery and death of those whom he encountered. For some, like the son of the widow of Nain and his friend Lazarus, Jesus' gift was resurrection from death; for others it was release from sin, like the woman caught in adultery. Still others, like those who daily walked the roads of Judea and Galilee with him, were given a new spirit, a whole new opportunity and way to encounter God. Jesus set all people free.

John Newton only realized his spiritual sickness when he came near to physical death during the great storm at sea. What will it take for us to discover our need for God? God rescued the Hebrews time and again as we read in the Scriptures. The Israelites were liberated from Egypt by Moses and the Judges defeated Israel's enemies in battle. The prophets, like Ezekiel, brought a message of new hope to the people if they would only heed God's law. God is ever active in our world. We have the Church, the Scriptures, and the example of many who have gone before us, marked by the sign of faith, who have conquered death and been raised to new life, to aid us in our journey home to God. Let us rise from our spiritual graves. Let us put on the armor of light which is Christ and continue our journey to Calvary, resurrection, and eternal life.

Passion/Palm Sunday

The Mission Of Christ Is Ours

Isaiah 50:4-9a

How does one define the concept of divinity? We might begin by some description of the aspects of being divine. The divine is infinite; the divine is omnipotent and omniscient. These ideas help to describe divinity, but they don't do much to define it. We need something to which we can relate, something common to our human experience, in order to understand the concept of the divine

The best answer to our original question for me is to speak in terms of participation in the divine. Thus, one can ask the question, how can one seek to be divine-like? An answer which appeals to me is: The degree to which we live for others is the degree to which we participate in the divine. We can give many examples of this idea. There is a dramatic example in the life of Saint Maximilian Kolbe. Kolbe was a Franciscan friar who ministered many years as a publisher and writer. During World War II he was sent to the Auschwitz concentration camp. One evening in the camp there was an attempted escape by one of the prisoners. The next morning the Nazi camp commander ordered that ten prisoners be randomly chosen and executed in retribution for the escape attempt and as a means to teach those held in the camp that such actions would not be tolerated. One of the men who was selected for execution was a Jewish family man whom Kolbe had befriended. Without regard to himself, the Franciscan priest volunteered to die in the other man's place. He gave his life so another could live.

Another dramatic example is one I witnessed on television several years ago during an episode of ABC's *Wide World of Sports*. The program covered the "Iron Man" competition, an annual test of strength, endurance, and courage held on the Hawaiian island of Oahu. Each competitor swims two miles in the open ocean, bikes over 150 miles over the highways of the island, and then finishes with a 26.2-mile marathon run. This particular year one competitor participated in and finished the event accompanied by his crippled son. For the two-mile ocean swim he towed his son behind him on a rubber raft. During the bike race his son sat in a specially-designed basket that rested on the bike's front handle bars. The man then ran the marathon with his son strapped to his back. When this competitor crossed the finish line to the road race, reporters, in awe of this accomplishment, asked why he had done it. The man very simply answered, "Because my son will never be able to do it." This father lived the experience of a lifetime for his son.

There are more famous examples of living for others. In his powerful "I Have a Dream" speech, proclaimed before hundreds of thousands gathered in the Washington Mall in August, 1963, Martin Luther King, Jr., expressed the hopes which he shared and lived for in creating a more just world for all. Until his tragic death in 1968 Dr. King continued to champion the cause of racial justice, living more for those he served than for himself. A couple years earlier John F. Kennedy, in his inaugural address, said, "Ask not what your country can do for you; ask what you can do for your country." He challenged the sensibility of our world which for too long has been centered on personal achievement and advancement. These famous Americans called the nation to a higher standard; they challenged us to live for each other.

There are incalculable routine and ordinary ways in which people live for others, yet maybe they are the most profound because they are everyday events: people who donate time to work in a soup line, a youngster who shares her sandwich with a child who has none, parents who sacrifice time, energy, and resources out of love for their son or daughter. These are simple and everyday occurrences, but they are profound examples of living for others. The extent to which we live for others is the extent to which we participate in the divine.

Our Lenten journey has reached its climax as we enter upon the most sacred time of the Church year — Holy Week. For five weeks we have prepared ourselves to celebrate the Paschal Mystery — the passion, death, and resurrection of Jesus — and now the time is upon us. In Jesus' personal Lent, his period of preparation, the climax came when he triumphantly entered Jerusalem, riding a donkey, with the people laying palm branches before him and shouting, "Hosanna." Jesus was welcomed to the great city as a hero, but his moment of victory and glory would be brief. The plot of the story will soon thicken, darkness will obscure the light, and the Son of God will suffer and die an ignoble death. Jesus went to the cross, his exaltation as Saint John understands the event, willingly; he lived for others until the very end. As members of the Christian community who daily strive to walk in the footsteps of the Lord, we are challenged to muster sufficient courage to follow Jesus' example of love and self-sacrifice.

Jesus' suffering was predicted long before he walked the roads of Israel. Isaiah prophesied, as we hear in today's reading, of one who would not rebel, but rather would allow the outrages perpetrated by humans to fall upon him. Scripture scholars refer to this passage in Isaiah as one of the "Suffering Servant" songs. The servant, a prophetic image of Christ, courageously endured the cruelty of an unbelieving, uncharitable, and hedonistic world, and he did so without fear. His face was set like flint with complete confidence that he would not be disgraced or put to shame. The servant was devoid of fear and possessed total confidence of victory because he knew that God, his help, refuge, and strength, was close at hand. Those who would oppose the servant will be confronted by God; the Almighty will be victorious. Thus, the servant could brave the indignation of others with the assurance that, in the end, God would uphold him and reward his righteous stand.

Christians today who live their faith forthrightly and openly will be challenged and most probably will face the anger and evil, manifest in various forms of pain, inflicted by those who are distant from God and/or society. Those in history and those we have known in daily life who lived for others were not afraid to enter into the lives of those they encountered each day. Similarly, the servant in Isaiah's prophecy did not avoid the conflicts or confrontations of life; he did not shield his face from buffets and spitting. The servant, Jesus, lived and ultimately died to set us free and bring us the possibility of eternal life.

We are challenged today, as we enter this sacred time in the church year, to reflect upon how we can better imitate those who have lived for others, people who in many ways have become Christ to the world. Life, society, and the material world are good; they are great gifts from God. But we all know that at times the world and its people can be cruel, even adversarial. We can hide from society and its challenges or, as the contemporary psychologist and writer Thomas More suggests in his book *Care of the Soul*, we can accept them and do our best to transform troublesome situations, events, and people into opportunities for personal and communal growth and the receipt of grace. Opportunities to change an attitude, transform anger, or correct injustice — in other words, to right the wrongs of the world — come in subtle and great ways, but generally with little or no warning. We must be ready when the challenge is presented; if we are not, the opportunity to bring a bit of conversion to our world will be lost. If we stay close to God, as we walk the road this Holy Week, then we can be confident that no matter what pain we experience, whether it comes from our mistakes or those of others, God will be present to sustain us. As the servant says, "He who vindicates me is near" (Isaiah 50:8a).

The road to resurrection is not easy. It is strewn with potholes and obstacles and has one major detour along the road; we cannot avoid the cross. But we must believe with utmost confidence that God will give us all that we need to reach the one important and ultimate goal of our life — union with the Lord. Thus, let us have the courage, like those who live for others, especially the Suffering Servant of Isaiah, to walk the road, confront the pain and suffering of the world, and continue our journey to death and to eternal life.

Maundy Thursday

Carrying On
The Tradition

Exodus 12:1-4 (5-10) 11-14

Tradition is an integral part of being human. All nations, peoples, cultures, and families celebrate many traditions in special and unique ways. In the United States there are many traditions, some of which have become so much a part of what we are as a nation that we don't even think of them as traditions. For example, we use a Roman form of law where the accused is considered innocent until proven guilty. Under our system of law people have rights guaranteed to them by the law of the land, the Constitution.

Summer is an annual event, a tradition, and a special time for all people. In our country there are certain summer events that are celebrated in traditional ways. Summer traditionally opens with the Memorial Day weekend. This is the time when people take that first trip out, go to vacation spots, or open summer homes to enjoy the better weather that lies ahead. Each summer we celebrate the national ritual of the Fourth of July with fireworks, parades, Uncle Sam, barbecues, and family outings to the park. It is a day when we proudly wear the red, white, and blue. The close of summer is traditionally celebrated over the Labor Day weekend. School will soon begin; vacations are over; it is time to settle in for the fall.

Tradition is an important element in the celebration of culture and ethnicity. On March 17 everyone is Irish at least in spirit. We wear green, eat corned beef and cabbage, watch a parade, and toast friends at a local pub. Ethnic groups celebrate the tradition of their language, customs, foods, saints, festivals, and holidays.

Families also celebrate their own traditions. Holidays such as Christmas, Easter, and Thanksgiving are often ritualized in families. It may be a trip to visit relatives, a dinner out, or a family gathering with Mom and Dad. Families many times celebrate birthdays, anniversaries, and other special events in ways which become traditions.

Tradition is certainly one of the key elements of all religion. Rituals and designated days to praise God, celebration of important events, and means to remember the past are all part of the tradition. Tonight the Christian community remembers the tradition and we celebrate our heritage as Judeo-Christian people.

The Jews, like all religious people, remember and celebrate the tradition of their ancestors. While the Jews remember many events of the past and practice traditions rich in history, there is none greater than the Passover, which we hear beautifully described in tonight's reading. God rescued the people; God saved them from the brink of death and brought them home to the land promised them many generations earlier. Jews celebrate the tradition of the seder meal when, as we heard, they ate roasted lamb and bitter herbs as a people in flight from bondage. The Passover, God's intervention on behalf of the people, is the central tradition of the Jews, and since Christianity finds its roots in Judaism it is appropriate that we hear this story tonight, when we enter into the central mystery and celebration of our Christian tradition.

Maundy Thursday is the beginning of the greatest celebration in the Christian tradition, the paschal mystery — the passion, death, and resurrection of the Lord. On this night we celebrate many traditions of our Christian heritage. We remember that it was this night that Jesus ate his last meal, a Passover meal, with his best friends, the apostles, who had walked the road with him from the beginning. At this meal Jesus gave us the Eucharist as a gift of his eternal presence with us. We also celebrate the tradition of community. We are gathered together as one Christian people to begin to walk more fervently with Jesus these last few hours before his salvific death. This is a night when we celebrate the Christian tradition of service, the common call for all baptized people to serve their brothers and sisters in love, responding to our God who first loved us.

We have many examples of Christian service which have carried on the tradition of Jesus. William and Catherine Booth founded the Salvation Army which even today serves millions of people with assistance and the Christian message. Dorothy Day and Peter Maurin founded the Catholic Worker Movement at the height of the Depression to provide shelter and a meal to those who lived on the streets of our cities. In a different but no less important way, Dietrich Bonhoeffer carried on the tradition of service by his fearless stance against Nazi tyranny and his refusal to forego the work for which he had been ordained.

All of us have been called by Our Lord, Jesus Christ, to live the tradition of the Church. We have been called to live in hope, a hope which only God can give. We are called to live in love and to express this most special yet difficult of human emotions to all. We are called to be servants, to others and to God.

Our Lenten journey from the desert to the tomb to resurrection has reached its climax; the three holy days are upon us. God rescued the Hebrew people from bondage when they cried out. Jesus Christ, God's only-begotten Son, has ransomed us from death by dying on the cross. The Hebrews celebrated the tradition of their rescue with a meal; we remember how God saved us with a meal of our own. Let us celebrate our tradition as people redeemed in God's love. Let us enter fully into these holy days, take the risk of dying a bit to self, so as to rise with Jesus to a new more glorious and eternal life.

Good Friday

Freely Sharing
The Burden

Isaiah 52:13—53:12

Once in a far-off land there was a great king whose dominion extended far and wide. His power and authority were absolute. One day a young man, a commoner, committed a grave offense against the king. In response the king and his counselors gathered together to determine what should be done. They decided that since the offense was so grave and had been committed by a commoner against someone so august as the king, the only punishment that would satisfy justice was death. The king's son, the crown prince, however, interceded on the young offender's behalf — you see, they were best friends. The prince spoke with his father and the counselors; the debate grew rather heated. In the end the king declared, "The offender must pay a price for his offense. I decree that he must carry a heavy burden up Temple Mountain. If he survives the ordeal he shall live!"

The prince again interceded for his friend. He knew the burden of which his father spoke was the weight of death and he knew his friend would not be able to carry it. Thus the prince declared, "Royal blood has been offended, therefore, only royal blood can pay the price." So the prince voluntarily shouldered the heavy burden himself, and with his friend trailing behind him, began the ascent of the mountain. The task was very difficult. The higher the prince climbed the heavier the burden became. The prince slipped and stumbled several times, but he always managed to right himself and keep going. When the two friends first saw the summit, their goal, the prince collapsed from sheer exhaustion. He said to his friend, "In order for justice to be served the price must be paid." The young man understood the prince and thus he shouldered the burden himself and, now with the prince following, managed to climb the rest of the way to the summit. When the two friends reached their goal, the prince, with his last ounces of strength, lifted the burden high over his head and then he died.

The king, observing all these events from below, declared, "Justice has been done." Then with his great power he returned his son to life. The prince, now returned to life, said, "Not so, not yet. Justice has not been served. Royal blood received help along the way!" The king had to agree. He pardoned the young offender and the two best friends lived happily ever after.[1]

Why does the world suffer? Why do pain, problems, and suffering exist in such abundance? We all believe that God is all good, all love, full of compassion, and all powerful. This is how we define God; we believe this is true. Thus, the question bears repeating, why does our world suffer? Why do wars exist and people die in innocence? Why do people in positions of public trust commit acts that cause others not only to lose faith in the individual, but in the system as well? Why do people fight one another and the only question between them is the color of their skin, their political preference, or their religious belief?

The answer to these challenging questions is personal choice, our free will which allows us to say yes or no to God at any time in any way. Sören Kierkegaard, the famous nineteenth-century existentialist philosopher and theologian, once wrote, "Faith is a matter of choice, our personal decision in finding God." This personal decision, our free will, is why the world suffers. It is free will that allows the drunk to drive and kill others. It is free will that allows people in public service to break the law and thus lower the integrity of the system. It is free will that places certain members and groups in society on the fringe and does not allow them to participate. Free will moves us closer to or further from God. As Kierkegaard wrote, it is our decision; faith is our choice.

Good Friday is obviously a day when we remember suffering and pain, but it is a day which has much more to offer. We remember Jesus' suffering, his pain, and eventual death; he was a victim of the cruelty of humanity. The great events of this day might easily lead us to ask, "Why did Jesus have to die?" The simple yet profound answer is that Jesus did not have to die; he chose to die, so that we could find life. Jesus' death came about of his own free will.

The reading from Isaiah, a "Suffering Servant" passage similar to the one we heard on Palm Sunday, speaks of the servant's free choice in dying. The appearance of the servant attracted no one; he was spurned, avoided by all, and accustomed to infirmity. He was a person of suffering and pain who bore our infirmities; he was pierced for our offenses and crushed for our sins. Like the prince in John Aurelio's story, he shouldered the great burden of life for us and he did it willingly, without our asking or a second thought on his part. As the servant gives his life, the will of God is accomplished through him. The sacrifice of the servant will win pardon for the offenses of others; his suffering will bring us to sanctification.

Free will is our gift from God, our ability to say yes or no. Our world suffers; Jesus suffers and dies. Both events happen through free choice. The prince used his gift of free will to carry the burden for his friend. He realized it was the weight of death which could not be born by his friend alone. Similarly Jesus' crucifixion shows us that free will, which has been used to create so much pain, can lead to good, good leading to love, and love leading to salvation. Jesus' example of free will, his demonstration of love, must be our choice as well. We might not be able to effect systemic change tomorrow, maybe not even in our lifetime. We can begin with ourselves, however, in following Jesus' law of love. Let us use our free will for good; let us use our free will for love by shouldering the burden of others. Let us use our free will to sacrifice, to die for others, and in the process be exalted with Jesus to an eternal life with God.

---

1. This story is paraphrased from John R. Aurelio, "The Burden: A Tale of Christ," in *Colors! Stories of the Kingdom* (New York: The Crossroad Publishing Company, 1993), pp. 130-132

Easter

Our Need To Talk With The Son

Acts 10:34-43

Three sisters lived in the forest. The oldest was named Bean Plant, the middle sister was Marigold, and the youngest's name was Lily. It was summer; the weather was beautiful and all who lived in the forest were happy and gay.

Bean Plant, the eldest sister, was one who attracted a lot of attention in the forest. She provided something that drew all the animals to her — the lush and rich beans which she produced so abundantly. All the squirrels, rabbits, and other animals came and ate their meals at Bean Plant's house. Bean Plant was proud; she found importance in what she produced and cared little for what others said or thought.

Marigold, the middle sister, was also very popular. She produced nothing of value, but she attracted a lot of attention nonetheless. The reason was that Marigold was radiantly beautiful. The gold, yellow, and orange blossoms which she produced brought her many suitors. They were all tall, dark, and handsome and had names of Spruce, Elm, and Oak. Marigold lived in her radiant beauty as the summer days passed.

The youngest sister, Lily, did not attract a lot of attention. She produced no fruit; she was not radiantly beautiful. Lily was short, skinny, and just plain green. Lily had one other habit which her sisters thought was odd; she was constantly talking with the sun. Each day when the sun would come up in the eastern sky Lily would say, "Good morning," and the sun would answer, "Good morning, I hope you slept well." Lily spoke with the sun at midday when the forest was warm from the sun's rays. She also spoke to her friend saying, "Good night, thanks for the day," when the sun would slip over the western horizon. Bean Plant and Marigold thought their sister was odd. "You can't speak with the sun," they insisted. But Lily would only answer, "Maybe yes, maybe no, but I will continue to talk with my friend the sun."

One day Lily came to her two older sisters in tears. "The sun is dying," she said. "The sun in dying." Now her sisters truly knew that Lily was crazy: "How can the sun be dying? It comes up every day and goes down each night. The sun is strong and powerful. How can it be dying? But, what of it?" the older sisters said. "We really don't need the sun after all." Yet, Lily insisted that it was true; the sun had told her so. Bean Plant and Marigold had to agree about a few things, however. The sun seemed to come up a little later and go down a little earlier each day. Additionally, they noticed that the sun was not as high in the sky as it had been earlier. "But what of it?" they said. "We don't really need the sun."

As the warmth of the summer months turned into the cooler months of autumn, Lily continued to speak with her friend the sun. Soon the winter began to come to the forest. The winds came and blew the beauty that once was Marigold all over the forest. Her suitors no longer thought her attractive. They lost their interest in her and their leaves as well. They decided to rest for the remainder of the winter. With the wind came the cold. The fruit which Bean Plant produced began to shrivel up; it was no longer attractive to the animals of the forest. They too decided to rest for the winter. One day the cold became so intense that Bean Plant was snapped off at the base; she was no more. But before the sun went away totally, it bent down and kissed its friend Lily and said, "I love you."

After a few months life once again began to appear in the forest. The snows melted and streams again began to run freely. Budding leaves appeared on the trees and the animals again began to forage for food. And there in the middle of the forest appeared one day the most beautiful snow-white Lily. As the sun peeked its head over the eastern horizon, Lily turned, opened her beautiful white flower, and said to her friend, "Thank you, I love you too."[1]

The story of Lily and her two sisters is obviously one of resurrection. But the tale tells us much more about the day we celebrate than the fact that one can rise from death; we learn about the traits and characteristics we need to foster in order to find resurrection and even more importantly how we must live as those redeemed by the Son. Lily was one who exhibited perseverance in her life and acted uprightly. What she said and did was testimony to her belief in the sun, the Son of God. She did not fear what others would think; she acted on what she knew was right in response to the sun, which nourished her in every way with all that was needed for life.

On Easter Sunday we come to church to remember an event, but more importantly we celebrate what that event did for all of us, God's children. The Easter event was witnessed by Peter, who had deserted Jesus, along with all the rest, in the Lord's greatest hour of need. But Peter, unfortunately, was even weaker than those who consciously stayed away. He wanted to find out what would happen, but when questioned about his association he denied knowing the Lord. Peter's denial wounded Jesus, but, because of his faith, it cut deeply into the apostle as well. Peter needed the resurrection to change him and it certainly did as we hear in today's reading from Acts. Besides his denial of Jesus, Peter, as we remember from the Gospels, was not in the beginning the great leader he became. When Jesus called him rock, Peter immediately disappointed the Lord by his inability to understand the Master's plan and his need to die. Peter many times fell short, but then came the resurrection and a new direction in life.

The picture we see of Peter today is that of a new man. Like Lily he is undeterred in his mission; his past fears evaporate, like the sun breaking through the morning fog. Peter is ready to go forth and proclaim how Jesus has touched his life. The apostle through the resurrection gained the strength to begin to realize his commission as a follower of Christ to go forth and continue his Master's work on earth. Jesus' call was not a mere invitation; it was a challenge in response to God who first loved him. Lily's relationship with the sun changed her and gave her new life. Peter's experience of the resurrection changed his relationship with Jesus, the Son, forever.

Easter must be for us much more than a miraculous event which happened nearly 2000 years ago. Jesus' triumph over death must change and transform us today. We must live as redeemed people who bask in the light of the resurrected Christ. Jesus' conquest of death has opened the door of eternal life for all who live today. This one event gave us the possibility of salvation, but how can Jesus' victory change us today?

Our common Christian vocation to holiness requires much of us, but passivity is not one of these qualities. We must be active in demonstrating the presence of Christ in our lives. If we leave this church today without the hope that Christ's resurrection can and must change us now, then we have missed one of the greatest opportunities of our lifetime.

What is our individual call? Each of us must answer for ourselves by looking inside. Peter was sent to preach, and we in different ways must do the same. Lily preached to her sisters, without their understanding or recognition by the way she spoke with the sun. We must preach to others, but it need not be like Peter's words; it may be like Lily's actions in communicating with the sun and refusing to bow to outside pressure to stop. All that we do witnesses to the power and presence of God in our lives. People observe us and make judgments. What do they see in us? Do others observe us, like Lily, talking with the sun, the Son of God, with our words and deeds, or do they receive another message from us?

Easter is an annual springtime event which raises hope that like the new growth present in nature we may bud forth new shoots in our lives. This can only happen, however, if we are willing to speak with the Son, Jesus, and ponder ways in which his resurrection, his conquest of death, can create a deep and lasting transformation in us. May the event of the resurrection enlighten and transform us to be better witnesses of God's love for the world; may it change us forever.

---

1. This story is paraphrased from "Lily," in Walter Wangerin, Jr., *Ragman and Other Cries of Faith* (San Francisco: Harper & Row, Publishers, 1984), pp. 44-52.

Easter 2

A Resumé For Resurrection

Acts 2:14a, 22-32

John Harding had it all; his credentials were impeccable. He had a wonderful family. His wife, Sally, was one of those people everyone enjoys meeting and instantly likes. His eight-year-old son, Rick, was a good student, enjoyed athletics, and obeyed his parents. John himself had moved up the corporate ladder. After graduating from Arizona State University, where he played baseball well enough to be offered a professional contract, he moved to California's "Silicon Valley" and signed on with one of the many software companies that operate in the region. Through his intelligence, diligence, and much hard work he rapidly moved into management, beginning at the bottom and moving up. Still in his thirties, national publications such as *Forbes*, *U.S.A. Today*, and *The Wall Street Journal* commented favorably on his managerial style. John Harding had the perfect resumé for life: academic achievement, awards, and many positions of importance.

With such a record it was not a big surprise when Millennium, the third largest software manufacturer in the world, offered Harding a special position; they asked him to be their chief executive officer. John jumped at the offer. Not only was it a great position, but it would allow him to return to his native New England. He settled in his home town of Boland, New Hampshire, only twenty miles or so from Concord, the world headquarters for Millennium.

Everything seemed to be going well for John. The town welcomed a favorite son; the company liked their new boss. Then in the twinkling of an eye everything changed for John Harding. Sally and Rick were riding in the family car. A drunk driver crossed the center line and an instant later they were both gone. John Harding had the perfect resumé for life; he had no resumé for death. Thus, in grief and shock he crawled into a shell of mourning and refused to come out.

After a couple of months an old friend, Bill West, came to John to see if he could pull him from his state of grief. He knew that John liked baseball; maybe he would consider being the manager of one of Boland's four summer Little League teams. Harding tried to run away, but Bill West was persistent, and so John agreed. His team was the Angels.

It was at this time that John Harding met little Timmy Noble. Timmy, a member of the Angels, was eight years old and a towhead just like his son Rick. Unlike his son, however, Timmy was not a good player; he did not have the gifts for baseball. He did not possess the keen eye to be a good hitter nor did he have the strong arm needed to be a good fielder. But Timmy Noble had some very important qualities nonetheless. He had courage and a big heart — how can one measure such qualities? He had determination and, most especially, Timmy Noble had faith.

The Angels did well that year; in fact, they won the League championship. Timmy Noble was not one of the stars; he just was not gifted as a baseball player. But there was something wrong, something radically wrong. Timmy Noble was very sick. He never told anyone; he never complained. He came to every practice and played in each game, even though he had to ride his bike five miles each way to the field. When the season was over and it was revealed that Timmy Noble had terminal cancer, John Harding knew the reason that God had led him to manage the Angels. John had the perfect resumé for life; Timmy Noble had the perfect resumé for eternal life.[1]

We live in a world today which demands that we have a good resumé. We need to have all the qualifications that will allow us the greatest opportunity, for employment and the many other avenues in life. In today's reading we hear a portion of the first missionary discourse of the Book of Acts. We are told the essential facts of the teaching that Jesus is the Christ — in other words we hear about Jesus' credentials, his resumé for life. In a short passage we are informed about Jesus' name, work, words, death, and resurrection; his life is described as one of signs, miracles, and wonders. We know from our reading of Scripture that this was true.

Jesus did many wonderful things that would look good on a resumé. He was a great teacher with an incredible ability to draw people to his "lectures." He was a miraculous healer which again attracted people from the whole region to his side. Yet, the greatest elements of his resumé might not be recognized as beneficial since they speak of his need for death and resurrection. Jesus' death, Luke tells us in this pericope, was integral to God's plan for human salvation. Seen in this light, Jesus' great sacrifice, which brought the possibility of eternal life to all people for all time, may have been the most valuable qualification he possessed and, therefore, the most important statement in his resumé. The Lord's resurrection also was central to God's plan. This event was predicted by David, Luke tells us, and formed the final chapter in a life totally lived for others. It was the closing element of his resumé which brought life to others.

The resumé which we write of our life, like that of John Harding, generally is fixed in the present in its description of everything that we can do. We spend a lot of time doing things that will make our resumé appear more attractive to others. In order to make ourselves physically more noticeable, we go to the gym, take laps around the track, and watch carefully what we eat. Educational credentials are critical to the resumé, and thus we obtain degrees by our attendance at the best schools. We realize that many times it is not what we know, but who we know, and thus we cultivate the "right" relationships which will one day pay off in our favor. Building a good resumé is important in our contemporary world; if we want to compete we must do our best to achieve the credentials that will be noticed by others.

Christians, however, must be building another resumé at the same time, one that has nothing to do with life today but everything to do with eternal life. Timmy Noble knew that his days were limited and he prepared himself and those around him for the eventuality that will come to all people. Yet, he was filled with hope, and thus lived his life to the fullest. His resumé would lead to death but eventually to resurrection. John Harding had all the credentials for life, but he needed to learn from his little player what was necessary to prepare more completely — for life today and death tomorrow.

The Easter season which we celebrate is a period when we contemplate the Lord's resurrection and ask how this one event of history can aid and transform us today. Jesus lived his life fully each day; he did not allow opportunity to pass by unnoticed. Yet, in building his resumé through, as Luke says, signs, wonders, and miracles, he was constantly preparing himself for the two greatest elements of his life, his salvific death for us and his conquest of death through resurrection. In a similar manner, we must learn to develop a resumé for eternal life as we construct one for life today. What credentials do we have? Are our qualifications limited to those that show up on the work resumé, the ones that society deems as essential for its needs? Or, can we say that we have made progress in gathering those elements of our life which can accept death, with the constant and sure hope that resurrection will follow? Our preparation must be for life and death; both are necessary to be fully ready.

Let us as the Easter season progresses reflect upon how Jesus lived his life for others through the resumé which he constructed. It was filled with many things that would make people stop and stare, but its most profound aspects were those ways he prepared for a death that would bring life to others. Let us imitate Jesus and die to self while we prepare our resumé for eternal life.

---

1. Synopsis of Og Mandino, *The Twelfth Angel* (New York: Fawcett Crest, 1993).

Easter 3

Metanoia: The Process Of Conversion

Acts 2:14a, 36-41

Is the life you lead one for which you want to be remembered? That very challenging and thought-provoking question certainly came to the mind of the famous Swedish scientist Alfred Nobel one day. In the common everyday exercise of reading the morning paper, Nobel discovered the challenge of God and the need for conversion before his very eyes.

Nobel was born in 1833 to a scientist and his wife. From his earliest days it was evident to everyone that Alfred was gifted intellectually. He read voraciously all that he could get his hands on; he excelled in literature. By the time he was fifteen he could read, write, and speak four languages besides his native Swedish. Although he showed promise in the "humanities," it was his love of science and his desire to be an inventor like his father that most excited him.

By his sixteenth birthday Nobel had exhausted the educational possibilities in his native district in Sweden. He decided to move away for more training. He first went to Paris and then across the Atlantic to the United States, where he spent four years studying science and engineering principles, ideas that had become that much more important after the onset of the Industrial Revolution in the latter decades of the eighteenth century.

With his education complete, Nobel returned to his native land and began to experiment in his laboratory, creating an invention or two, but nothing of any significance. In the 1860s, however, he began to conduct experiments with nitroglycerin, a highly volatile and unstable substance. One experiment created an explosion in which Alfred's younger brother was killed. The experience crushed Nobel in one way, but in another it was the catalyst to find a way to harness the energy of this substance and make it of practical use to the world.

Nobel discovered a functional use of nitroglycerin, but it came quite accidentally. One day in his workshop, he noticed that some of the nitroglycerin, which is a liquid, had leeched into some packing material which surrounded the many bottles of chemicals sent him for his various experiments. Nobel found that this third substance, made from the initial two, had all the energy capacity and blasting potential of nitroglycerin, but it was stable and thus could be controlled. Without knowing it, Alfred Nobel had invited dynamite.

The uses of dynamite throughout the world made Nobel a rich and famous man overnight. Mountains could be blasted away to make room for railroads. Of equal use, however, was the placement of dynamite in bombs, projectiles, and other weapons of war. With patents received in 1867 and 1868, first in the United States and later in Great Britain, for dynamite and blasting caps, Nobel gained great notoriety. With the discovery of oil on land he owned in the state of Russia, Nobel became one of the richest men in the world. He could sit back, relax, and enjoy life.

Alfred's serenity came to an abrupt halt one day when he picked up the morning paper. The headline read, "Dynamite King Dies." The story and obituary in the paper were erroneous; he was very much alive and well. Nobel decided to read the article, however, in order to know what people would think of him after his death. Besides all the normal facts and dates of an obituary, Nobel read a description which labeled him as the "merchant of death." The expression disturbed the scientist greatly. Certainly the comment came in reference to his association with dynamite, but this did not lighten the blow. Nobel realized at that moment that the life he had led was not one for which he wanted to be remembered. He needed to change.

Something needed to be done to correct this situation. The past was history; its record was etched in stone. The future was something, however, over which Nobel had some control. Alfred was a rich man. How, he thought, could that money be put to a positive use? He decided to change his will and leave his vast fortune in trust to a committee which would select people annually who, in theory and practice, had made positive contributions to the furthering of humankind. Thus, in 1901, five years after his death, the first Nobel Prizes were awarded, initially in five areas: physics, chemistry, literature, medicine, and the famous Nobel Peace Prize. Later, in 1968 and thereafter, a prize in economics was added.

Alfred Nobel experienced conversion. God challenged him in many ways, but he never took the time, nor realized the significance of God's presence. After reading a false obituary, he was determined not to allow the presence of God to pass him by again!

Saint Peter, as the Acts of the Apostles clearly shows, was a different person after the resurrection. He was the same physical man but God had led him to conversion. Now it was his turn to lead others to their need for *metanoia* or change of heart. Peter challenged his fellow Jews to believe that Jesus was the promised Messiah, whom the people had long awaited, by shocking them. He tells them that they had responsibility in Jesus' death. Those who received this revelation openly sought a way to respond: "Brothers, what shall we do?" Peter tells them that they need to repent, to change their attitude and actions, and to be baptized. This *metanoia* or change of heart will lead to the remission of sins and will place them on the road to union with God. Peter further informs the people that conversion is their choice: "Save yourselves from this corrupt generation" (Acts 2:40b). God will give all people every opportunity to be transformed but the choice is always left to us.

Alfred Nobel, shocked by his description as "the merchant of death," changed overnight and will always be remembered for his promotion of intellectual pursuit. The Jews were challenged by Peter to seek conversion and discover through baptism the ways of Jesus. What will it take for us to find *metanoia*, change of heart, in our lives?

We all require conversion, the need to change attitudes and actions in our lives, but it will not happen overnight. Conversion is an on-going process. We might be able to say and truly mean that we have been converted, that we have given our life to the

Lord and rejected sinful ways of the past. But we need always to be open to change and conversion; the dynamism of the world will not allow us to remain staid in any aspect of our lives. However, we hope we will not need to read a false obituary or feel the guilt with which Peter challenged his fellow Jews to know our need to enter this journey of *metanoia*.

Conversion in our lives comes in many forms. We must seek conversion in our attitudes — to be more inclusive with all people, especially those we don't know or with whom we choose not to associate. We must learn greater tolerance of opinions while always upholding what is right in the eyes of God. We must seek transformation in our actions, always thinking before we speak or act. When we realize that what we do and say speaks to others of our beliefs and priorities, the importance of our actions and our need to execute them prudently becomes crystal clear. Conversion in method, how we do and say things, is also required. Confrontation, reprimand, and correction are many times the best response to a situation, but we can conduct ourselves in an angry and bitter way or with conciliation and gentleness. The method we use will make all the difference in the world in the final outcome.

During the Easter season we celebrate resurrection and rebirth. Baptism, the mark that signs us as Christians, is our sacramental conversion, but we all must continue on a daily basis to be re-baptized through a process of conversion, *metanoia*, our change of heart. The ways of society vie for our attention and can be a powerful temptation which draw us away from the Christian principles we hold and profess. Those who accept the power of Christ's resurrection need not wait for death to experience new life; it can be found today in our desire for conversion and the way we are drawn closer to God. Let us be open to change and not require some shock, like the experience of Alfred Nobel, to be converted. If we can experience *metanoia*, a change of heart each day, we will draw closer to Jesus and in the end find eternal life.

Easter 4

Community Forms
The Common Good

Acts 2:42-47

"**Outlined** against a blue-gray October sky, the Four Horsemen rode again. In dramatic lore they are known as pestilence, famine, destruction, and death. These are only aliases. There real names are Stuhldreher, Miller, Crowley, and Layden." Grantland Rice, a well-known sports columnist in an earlier era, wrote those memorable words one Saturday in October 1927. With these words a legend was started, for college football, for the immortal coach Knute Rockne and, that day especially, for the Four Horsemen of Notre Dame.

Who were the Four Horsemen? Elmer Layden, Harry Stuhldreher, Jim Crowley, and Don Miller were the talented offensive backfield for the Notre Dame football team in the late 1920s. There is no doubt that they were great players. Football fans then and now remember their names and their exploits on the gridiron. All four have been enshrined in the College Football Hall of Fame.

Most people know, however, that there are eleven players on a football team. What about the other seven? Who were they; what did they do? History knows them as the "Seven Mules." Few if anyone remembers their names; none of them are members of the College Football Hall of Fame. Still, I am certain that the Four Horsemen knew them. In fact, the same Grantland Rice who immortalized the Horsemen said that this talented backfield attributed all their success to the Mules. They were the ones who stood in front, did the blocking, ran interference, and cleared a path for the two halfbacks, the fullback, and the quarterback to run the plays, score touchdowns, and bring victory to Notre Dame.

The Four Horsemen and the Seven Mules were a team. They knew that they needed each other. Without the Mules the Horsemen probably would have been an ordinary college football backfield. But the combination of the Mules and the Horsemen brought greatness, fame, and legend to Miller, Layden, Crowley, and Stuhldreher and to Notre Dame football as well.

The lesson illustrated by the teamwork of the Four Horsemen and Seven Mules was learned and practiced by the first Christians from the outset. These disciples of Jesus were a very small minority who lived in a world which was quite hostile to their belief and way of life. Their new-found faith placed them at odds with most everyone in society, and thus they banded together to find the strength and the courage to do the work which was their commission as followers of the Lord. Jesus had been very specific as we remember, "Go therefore and make disciples of all nations, baptizing them in the name of the Father and of the Son and of the Holy Spirit, and teaching them to obey everything that I have commanded you" (Matthew 28:19). Acts today tells us that these Christians held all things in common, were devoted to the instructions of the apostles, and lived a communal life. They came to realize, possibly by experience or by revelation, that as individuals they would not go far, but as a group which pooled their unique and important gifts they could not only survive but expand and flourish. Thinking and acting for the group instead of the individual became a way of life for the people.

Today's society stresses the individual to the point, many times, of selfishness. We are trained, almost from birth, that we must get ahead, push in front of others, at almost any cost. We must do our best to beat the competition which becomes more intense day by day. The concept of the common good does not seem to be very popular these days; it certainly is not the priority of those who dominate our headlines. At every turn of life we encounter the individual triumphant over the whole. Teamwork in sports is utilized to enhance the possibilities of the individual. People in political life spend as much time working for re-election as they do for the constituents who elected them. Business aims to increase profits of a few at the expense of the majority whose efforts built the company. In short, we have rearranged our priorities and the common good has become the loser.

Our world needs a greater sense of community — people living, working, and praying together. This transformation must begin with our attitudes. How can our actions and words benefit all and not just ourselves or a select few? When we begin to think along lines that go beyond ourselves then we can change our actions to be consistent with our new thought. Thinking of others might be perceived as self-sacrifice, but we will find that when each person contributes his or her special gift, the total is greater than the sum of the individual parts. There is no sacrifice; what we attain is greater than we could ever possibly accomplish alone.

Community as a form of teamwork will give us strength and bring us to victory and prosperity, as happened with the Four Horsemen and Seven Mules and with those first Christians in Jerusalem. We must build communities in our neighborhoods. In today's lifestyle we often do not even know our neighbors, but the trend can and must be reversed. Some communities organize to form neighborhood watch programs; others celebrate holidays with block parties. Christian community is also forming in beautiful ways. People gather to read and reflect upon the Scriptures or to form prayer circles. In Latin America base Christian communities *(communidades de base)* serve to bring people together so they can share their faith.

Today the world emphasizes the individual but at times to the detriment of the whole. As God's children we have been individually and uniquely created by God and thus possess a special dignity. But as important as our individual worth and dignity are, they will find their greatest value and usefulness when they are combined with the goodness and talent of others to form a joint effort. Community was the life blood of the early Christians; it must be the same for us today. Let us work as a team in our common vocation to holiness. Let us build our Christian community so that others may say of us as they said of those first followers of Jesus, "See how they love one another."

Easter 5

Proclaiming The Message Of God

Acts 7:55-60

"**When** Christ calls a person, he bids that one to come and die." These words were written by Dietrich Bonhoeffer, a well-known Lutheran pastor and theologian, in a book influential to many, *The Cost of Discipleship*, first published in 1937. Bonhoeffer lived his Christian call to holiness without counting the cost. He did what God asked of him and he did it without qualification, reservation, or question. He did not look over his shoulder and wonder why, rather he lived what he wrote. Discipleship, if lived fully, would cost him his life.

Bonhoeffer was born in the state of Prussia in 1906. He grew up in an academic environment near the University of Berlin where his father was a professor of neurology and psychiatry. Later in his own study of theology he became interested in the historical-critical method of Adolph von Harnack and was a disciple of Swiss theologian Karl Barth who promoted the new "theology of revelation." After completing his doctorate, Bonhoeffer in 1931 spent one year at New York's Union Theological Seminary in a post-doctorate fellowship and exchange program. Returning to Germany he resumed duties which he had begun earlier as a pastor and writer.

In 1933, however, things changed for Bonhoeffer, the German people, and ultimately the world with the rise of the Nazi regime and Adolf Hitler. Bonhoeffer was one of the first and certainly the most vocal opponent of the Nazi ideology of anti-Semitism. Between 1935 and 1940 Bonhoeffer headed an underground seminary for Germany's "Confessing Church" (even though it was proscribed in 1937) which led the German Protestant resistance to Hitler. He was able to continue his work as pastor and theologian in the early war years under cover as a member of the military intelligence community. Bonhoeffer believed that the root evil for many of society's problems was a lax attitude toward morality which he said was fostered by the ready distribution of "cheap grace" to members of the Church. He was an ecumenist and promoted his belief in speeches and writings.

In April 1943 Bonhoeffer's books, essays, and talks led to his arrest for insurrection. He was ordered imprisoned, but this only strengthened his beliefs. It was at this time that he wrote his most famous work, *Prisoner of God: Letters and Papers from Prison*. Implicated in a failed July 1944 plot to assassinate Hitler, Bonhoeffer was transferred to a concentration camp in Flossenberg, Bavaria, where on April 9, 1945, only days before the Allied liberation of the camp, he was executed. Dietrich Bonhoeffer died for the Christian beliefs which formed his life; he was a martyr who never counted the cost.

Our reading today challenges us, like the words of Dietrich Bonhoeffer, and asks, "How much are we willing to pay to follow the Lord?" Stephen was called forth from the early Christian community, along with six other men, to serve the needs of those who were being neglected. He was called, like Dietrich Bonhoeffer, to answer God's call in his life; he never counted the cost in his response. Somehow Stephen understood that discipleship was a call to complete commitment; a half-hearted effort was not acceptable.

It did not take long for the zealous Stephen to lock horns with the Jewish authorities over the message of Jesus. Stephen was fearless in his denunciation of the Jews, whom he described as "stiff-necked people, uncircumcised in heart and ears," and "forever opposing the Holy Spirit." He claims that the people killed the prophets and recently Jesus as well. The law was given to the Jews but they failed to heed its message. Many tried to engage Stephen in debate and refute his arguments, but Luke tells us that none possessed the wisdom and spirit present in Stephen.

Luke portrays Stephen as similar to Jesus in his courage, accusation by the Jews, and eventual ignoble and painful death. Stephen is accused of uttering blasphemies and speaking against the law, and of violations of Mosaic custom, as was Jesus earlier. Although he was accused, Stephen is never convicted and thus his death at the hands of the mob could accurately be described as a lynching. Stephen realized that he would not fair any better than his master, the one he chose to serve and for whom he would die.

Few if any of us will ever be asked, like Dietrich Bonhoeffer or Stephen, to give our lives for what we believe, but all of us must make the commitment of these men (and others we have known) to secure the faith necessary to do what God asks and never count the cost. Each of us is challenged in different ways to speak out fearlessly and to refuse to accept attitudes and policies which draw us away from God. We must be the voice in the desert and the light in a sea of darkness.

The message of Christ must be applied to our personal lives and the world in which we live. We are called to speak against the injustice which is rampant in our society and threatens individuals and groups alike. We must be willing to make a stand against the forces of evil which seek to transgress Jesus' message of love. We might think ourselves only a small voice in a large crowd, but if many people band together great strength can be found and results achieved. Our call is to refuse to cooperate with corrupt or unjust practices which seek to achieve some goal at the expense or destruction of people. We must also reject compromise with the world. Dietrich Bonhoeffer and Stephen remained aloof from the forces of darkness which sought to neutralize their values and efforts; they refused to compromise their commitment to proclaim fearlessly God's message in the world.

Discipleship is not an easy road; it will be filled with many obstacles, ruts, and detours; there will be pain along the way. But, like Stephen, we can expect no better than the master we follow. Jesus suffered greatly, yet he never compromised his teachings or actions to accommodate others. We who bear the name Christian will also find suffering along the road to the Father. But if we can courageously continue on our path then the reward of eternal life will be ours.

May we be inspired to continue to walk with the Lord during this Easter season. We can live with total confidence that the hope of resurrection which we all possess is not void of content. God is always present to illumine the darkness of our world. Let us bear witness as Jesus' disciples to the power of Christ's resurrection in our lives!

Easter 6

Center Yourself In The Lord

Acts 17:22-31

When Charlie Atlas was a teenager his parents purchased for him a dresser mirror that he placed in his bedroom. Before this, whenever Charlie needed to use a mirror, he went to the bathroom, but there he was only able to see his head and possibly his shoulders. When he got dressed up he used his parents' full-length mirror in their bedroom. Charlie was happy with his new mirror; he spent many hours in front of it.

One day, while standing in front of the mirror, Charlie decided to take off his shirt. He was very disappointed. His chest was scrawny and his biceps were so thin that he could place his hand completely around one. This was an intolerable situation; he did not want to be known as a scrawny weakling. Thus, on that very day Charlie Atlas made a pact with himself. He would work as hard as necessary in order to build up his upper body, so that he would not be embarrassed before the mirror ever again. Thus, Charlie began a rugged daily regimen of exercise. For several hours each and every day he did exercises — push-ups, pull-ups, and sit-ups. Later he began to lift weights, barbells, and dumbbells. He bought a special machine with weights, pulleys, and springs which allowed him to work out harder. He even used hand grips when he was relaxing to strengthen his forearms.

After several months Charlie again looked in the mirror. There was definite improvement. His chest had grown and his arms were more muscular. The positive results he achieved encouraged him and thus he doubled his efforts. He did more difficult exercises, lifted heavier weights, and now even began to eat only certain foods.

He took lots of vitamins as well. After a few years of this strenuous exercise program, Charlie again looked in the mirror. He was quite satisfied, even elated. His chest was huge and taut. His biceps were so large that one could not use two hands in attempting to encircle one; his stomach rippled like the waves on the ocean. As he stood in personal admiration, all of a sudden Charlie collapsed. His parents were quite concerned and rushed him to the doctor. They thought for certain that it was a case of over exertion, but after examining Charlie, the doctor said it was much more simple. Charlie's ankles and legs were too weak, they could not support his massive bulk, thus he collapsed. You see, Charlie could only see his upper body in the mirror and that was all he developed.[1]

In different ways we are all Charlie Atlases. Few of us spend the time he did in building our bodies, but we do spend lots of time working on the externals in our lives, our physical condition, mind, appearance, and job. In some ways these become the gods which we worship. We live in the here and now and concern ourselves with that which is present before us. But like Charlie Atlas, as well, we fail many times to build up the foundation, that which is most basic in our lives. For we who bear the name Christian, our foundation must be our relationship with God.

Saint Paul, in his travels around the Mediterranean world, encountered Gentiles who practiced idolatry, the worship of false gods. Such had been the practice of the all the great civilizations in human history — the Egyptians, Babylonians, and now the Greeks and the Romans. Each of these peoples developed their own pantheon with gods "manufactured" by the human mind to explain the created world and the events of daily life. Paul found his opportunity to enter into discussion with the Athenians when he discovered a temple to "an unknown god." Paul used the occasion to point to the fallacy of the Greeks' worship of gods generated and fashioned by human hands. For the Greeks and the other civilizations of the pre-Christian world, gods were made visible in stone or metal, but Paul says that the true God has created us to search for Him. Certainly the God of whom Paul speaks is different than any other god. The true God has fixed a day when the world will be judged by the one appointed to the task, Jesus, who was raised from the dead.

Paul preached against the practice of idolatry, which was the common experience of the people; but his message, at least in this instance, was not well received. There were a few who heard the voice of God in Paul's words and reformed their lives and sought repentance. Contemporary civilization is highly advanced and the thought might be held that idolatry no longer exists. As a sophisticated people and advanced civilization we read the mythology of the Greeks and the Romans for its literary value but wonder how people could have been so blind as to generate a complete system of gods for each and every occasion and need.

As bright, articulate, and advanced as we might perceive ourselves to be, however, many times we practice idolatry and don't even realize it. Our pantheon is filled with contemporary names such as money, material possessions, power, prestige, position, appearance, and name. Like Charlie Atlas, who spent all his time developing the externals of his physical body which he could see in the mirror, we spend much time and energy engaged in the pursuit of excellence and perfection as we search for today's false gods. How much time do we spend in the pursuit of our relationship with the true God, who created all, and His Son, Jesus Christ? Do we realize our need to build up the rock foundation of our life — our relationship with God?

There is a need to build up the externals of our life. If we do not take the time to cultivate our minds, to gain competence in our field, then the world will pass us by; we will be figuratively "run over" by the competition. If we neglect to care for our bodies then the time we have on this earth will probably be less and of poorer quality. If we are given opportunities to use our talents for the betterment of ourselves and our world and refuse to participate, then we have misused God's gifts. Yet, as important as the externals of our lives are, if we fail to nurture our relationship with God, then most assuredly, like Charlie Atlas, we will stand tall and then one day suddenly collapse without warning.

Idolatry, unfortunately, is alive and well; it did not die with modern society but rather changed the names of its gods.

Contemporary life demands much of us — our time, expertise, and material possessions. The tendency, with all the hurdles of life, is to take the easy, clearly-marked route, the one most traveled. This route, however, many times leads us astray from the goal that we seek. Even worse paths, individuals, ideologies, or events which we choose to solve the problems we face too often become the things that gain our allegiance; they become our own pantheon. This cannot be for those who profess to be disciples of Jesus Christ.

In the maze of life it is easy to get off track and find some dead ends. We need a guide to reach our goal. Jesus is the guide and the goal. He has explained both well as related by Saint Matthew the evangelist in the Sermon on the Mount: "Enter through the narrow gate; for the gate is wide and the road is easy that leads to destruction, and there are many who take it. For the gate is narrow and the road is hard that leads to life, and there are few who find it" (Matthew 7:13-14).

---

1. Paraphrased from "Charlie Atlas and the Dresser Mirror," in John R. Aurelio *Colors! Stories of the Kingdom* (New York: The Crossroads Publishing Company, 1993), pp. 26-27.

Ascenson Of The Lord

Completing The Master's Work

Acts 1:1-11

Giacomo Puccini was one of the greatest composers of opera who ever lived. His great and glorious music, written for and performed in the great opera houses of the world, has delighted people for more than a century. Puccini was given many great gifts by God, but certainly the greatest was his musical ability. He gained great fame, not only in his native land of Italy, but throughout the world. It was quite common to hear people along the streets of any great city whistling or humming one of the many popular melodies from such great works as *Tosca, La Boheme, Madama Butterfly, Manon Lescaut,* and *Gianni Schicchi.*

Toward the end of his life Puccini took on a challenge, the composition of another great opera. Using a libretto written by fellow Italian Renato Simoni, who adapted a work of the eighteenth-century Venetian playwright Carlo Gozzi, Puccini tackled the composition of *Turandot,* the story of a gallant young man, Calaf, in his efforts to win the hand in marriage of the stern, mysterious, and seemingly cold Chinese princess named Turandot. Puccini was in his sixties when he began the opera's composition. For four years he labored long and hard, but Puccini was a very sick man. He was running out of time; God would soon call him home.

Puccini did return home to God, but his master work was not completed. Because he was a famous man, Puccini had many friends, including a cadre of loyal students who were known as his disciples. These young men and women would not allow their master's great work, his *magnum opus,* to lie unfinished. Thus, they gathered together, studied the text of the opera, and then began the difficult task of finishing their master's work. In 1926, two years after his death, Puccini's greatest work, *Turandot*, was performed for the first time, appropriately enough at Milan's La Scala Opera House with Arturo Toscanni, the most famous conductor of the day, at the podium. When the opera reached the point where Puccini's work ended Toscanni paused, set down his baton and said, "Thus far the master wrote, but he died." After a moment of silence Toscanni again picked up his baton, turned to the audience, and with tears in his eyes said, "But his disciples finished his work." To thunderous applause the opera continued; the work of the master had been completed.

In some important ways Giacomo Puccini's life paralleled that of Jesus. Christ was sent by God to be with us for a certain amount of time; he was sent on a mission. Like Puccini, who was sent by God to delight our ears with beautiful music, so Jesus was sent to show us how to lead good and holy lives, to demonstrate the presence of God in the world. Jesus was given many wonderful gifts by God the Father in order to carry out his special mission on earth. Without question Jesus was the greatest teacher of all time. He taught us the most important lessons of life — how to love and to care for others by leading lives of service. Jesus was a worker of miracles. He raised the dead to new life, including his good friend Lazarus and the only son of the widow of Nain, and brought sight to the blind, hearing to the deaf, and mobility to the crippled. He even cured those who at least in theory did not believe in him, such as the son of the Roman centurion. Maybe most importantly, Jesus was one who forgave others and taught us to forgive. He forgave Saint Peter, who denied him three times, and went so far as to forgive those who nailed him to the cross and sent him to an ignominious death: "Father, forgive them for they know not what they are doing" (Luke 23:24).

Jesus came to our world with a special mission. He wanted to show by what he did and said that God is not far away, but rather, God is close, imminent; God is present within ourselves and our society. Jesus came to establish the Kingdom of God on earth, but he returned home before the mission was completed. As we hear in the Acts of the Apostles, Jesus ascended to heaven; he went back home to God. We who bear Christ's name are his friends, disciples, and students. When Puccini died without his master work completed his disciples gathered together and finished the work. In a similar way, we who bear the name Christian must do our share to bring Jesus' work to completion in our world.

God has given all of us many talents and we must use them to bring the Kingdom to come. Some, like Puccini, are gifted musically; others are writers; still others are talented speakers. Some of us excel in science and others are exceptional teachers. Some people have been given great athletic ability and some of God's people are very fortunate — they have been blessed with multiple talents. Whatever gifts we have received from God must be returned in our effort to make known to others the imminence of God in our world. We must show others that love conquers hate, that faith dispels fear, and that community can take us further than personal initiative alone. We must do our share to build the Kingdom now.

Jesus ascended to heaven and returned to the Father, but we, his disciples, are still here. As missionaries on the road, God has granted us limited time. For some the time is 25 years, for others sixty, and for a select few one hundred. Each and every day of our journey presents the opportunity to show the face of God to others, to complete Jesus' work in building the Kingdom of God. Let us do our share as we walk in the footsteps of the master. Let us build the City of God this day!

Easter 7

The Community Of Life

Acts 1:6-14

Unity and disunity — these words are more than mere opposites. Certainly when unity exists things are together; where disunity reigns things are apart. There is more, however, to understanding these terms. Unity is something that is quite natural. It is the flow of nature, for humans and the world in general. Unity is something we seek; it does our world good to seek and find unity. Disunity, on the other hand, is seldom found in nature. Disunity is unnatural and not desired by humans; disunity is to be avoided.

Since unity is that which we desire, we need to find images that help us to picture this idea. One good example is alloy metals. Alloys are mixtures of two dissimilar metals which when united form a third substance which is stronger, longer lasting and more durable than either of the original two metals from which it is made. Energy is needed to bind the metals into a specific lattice structure so that they can possess the qualities needed for our specific applications. Rivers are another example of the unity in nature. Tributaries of a river flow into the whole. The larger river is stronger, deeper, and more useful than the tributaries from which it is formed. The boundaries of the river, its banks, hold it together, allowing it to flow freely and sustain much life in the process.

Humans seek unity as well. The peoples of nations seek unity. We live in the United States, a group of fifty sovereign or independent states. Yet these individual states choose to band together as one. What binds them together is the law of the land, the Constitution. In the United States the charism of the Declaration of Independence, which says, "All people are created equal," also binds us together. Nations band together in international groups such as the United Nations, NATO, and a host of similar world bodies. Humans seek unity in a more generic sense through the concept of community. It may be a neighborhood watch group, a community-action organization, or even a religious community of men or women. The bond here is the common issue, the common commitment, or the common way of life. The Church is a community of faith where people come to worship, gain strength, and live more fully.

Jesus gathered a community of twelve apostles as the base of what became the Church. These men walked the road with the Lord, heard his words, and witnessed his many miracles. They were entrusted with a mission to spread Jesus' message of love and peace to all people. The apostles were a group united by the presence of Jesus. But as the Lord prepared to leave our world and return to the Father the apostles were faced with the need to continue the work, a daunting task without their leader. The mission was even more complex since the unity of the apostles had been broken. Judas, as Scripture says, was destined to be the Lord's betrayer, to go his own way. Although his loss was predicted, it created a rupture in the unity, which needed to be repaired. Thus, the apostles huddled together and began truly to understand through its lived experience the beauty and power of community.

Luke in this section of the Acts of the Apostles tells us that those first Christians gathered together in prayer to seek the strength that they needed to persevere in a difficult world, an environment which was often hostile to their presence. Jesus had taught these men the value of community during his public ministry. The Lord did not operate alone, but rather taught and performed his many magnificent signs in the presence of those whom he had gathered when he first left Galilee. The apostles huddled together without their leader out of fear, a normal human reaction in such circumstances; they knew the community was their source of strength. In an unfriendly world they began to count on others to share their joys, burdens, fears, and pains. They welcomed into their group others who shared their beliefs and had walked the road with Jesus, including women who had been in their company from the beginning.

We must seek unity in our lives, both within our own person and with those whom we encounter in our daily lives. Community, the unity we seek, is an integral aspect of the Christian call to holiness. We do not walk the road of faith alone; we walk with other pilgrims and in this way discover strength for the journey. Today we often hear people say, "If you want it done right, do it yourself." This statement is expedient; it often saves us time, which is in far too short supply. We mistakenly think, however, that if we do it ourselves it will be done correctly and efficiently. Our statement indicates a lack of trust in another and an unwillingness on our part to allow a person to enter into our lives. We present an attitude of personal isolation. We say in effect, "I don't need you." The reality is, however, that although the task might be completed more slowly and with less efficiency the first time another tackles it, things will eventually be better and (in the end) time saved since we will not need to complete the task or have the responsibility. If we can take the time now to teach another how to complete a task, we aid that person and more importantly build the community that we so desperately need. We make a great mistake when we perceive ourselves to be invincible, that we can "go it alone" without the love and support of others.

How do we build community? What is the glue that holds different people together and allows them to act as a unity of one? The answer most assuredly is love. Love is a small word, but we all know that it is very complex. The ancient Greeks, a very intelligent and highly civilized society, also realized that love was a complicated idea. In philosophy and in language the Greeks used three different words to express the concept of love, realizing its complexity. The first type of love for the Greeks was *phileo*, brotherly and sisterly love, which is expressed between siblings and best friends. The second word was *eros*, romantic love, expressed between one man and one woman. This type of love is centered in self. Although we may give much to the one we love, *eros* is an emotion which is self-satisfying. This is a personal need which all people feel and desire. The third form of love, and for the Greeks the highest expression, is *agapao*, commonly known as agape. This is the love that we outwardly express in our service, ministry, and relations with others. Agape is centered on the other, not the self. It is, therefore, a special and powerful love which is rooted in the Christian understanding of faith and Jesus' message of love and service.

Agape must be the expression of our lives in our relationships with others. This must be the glue which binds our community together, giving strength and making us one in our common task to carry out Jesus' mission in our world. There will be many obstacles and hurdles in our personal and communal lives of faith, but with the bond of love for God, one another, and the mission that we undertake, we can negotiate them and find ourselves as individuals and community stronger because of the trial.

As followers of Jesus we have been commissioned through baptism to live lives of holiness, service, and ministry. We must not act alone but within the community of the Church which will give us the purpose for our efforts, the strength to endure, and the peace that only the Lord can give. Let us wrap ourselves and those we know in the blanket of God's love which unites the Christian community, making us one in purpose, motive, and action. May the example of the those first Christians, the apostles and their friends, empower us to seek unity and peace in the bond of community with Christ Jesus as our capstone and source of light, love, and peace.

Books In This Cycle A Series

GOSPEL SET

And Then Came The Angel
Sermons for Advent/Christmas/Epiphany
William B. Kincaid, III

The Lord Is Risen! He Is Risen Indeed! He Really Is!
Sermons For Lent/Easter
Richard L. Sheffield

No Post-Easter Slump
Sermons For Sundays After Pentecost (First Third)
Wayne H. Keller

We Walk By Faith
Sermons For Sundays After Pentecost (Middle Third)
Richard Gribble

Where Gratitude Abounds
Sermons For Sundays After Pentecost (Last Third)
Joseph M. Freeman

FIRST LESSON SET

Between Gloom And Glory
Sermons For Advent/Christmas/Epiphany
R. Glen Miles

Cross, Resurrection, And Ascension
Sermons For Lent/Easter
Richard Gribble

Is Anything Too Wonderful For The Lord?
Sermons For Sundays After Pentecost (First Third)
Leonard W. Mann

The Divine Salvage
Sermons For Sundays After Pentecost (Middle Third)
R. Curtis and Tempe Fussell

When God Says, "Let Me Alone"
Sermons For Sundays After Pentecost (Last Third)
William A. Jones

SECOND LESSON SET

Moving At The Speed Of Light
Sermons For Advent/Christmas/Epiphany
Frank Luchsinger

Love Is Your Disguise
Sermons For Lent/Easter
Frank Luchsinger

www.ingramcontent.com/pod-product-compliance
Lightning Source LLC
Chambersburg PA
CBHW071741040426
42446CB00012B/2418